The Art of Christian Warfare

■ ■ ■

Rules of Command

By Prince Handley

University of Excellence Press

UNIVERSITY OF EXCELLENCE PRESS
Los Angeles ■ London ■ Tel Aviv

ISBN-13: 978-0692263839
ISBN-10: 0692263837

Printed in the U.S.A.

First Edition

✠

The only book you need on Christian Warfare

TABLE OF CONTENTS

FOREWORD

If you want to reach **the whole world** for Messiah Jesus, this is the book you need. Fashioned in the foundry of the Holy Spirit and forged on the anvil of prayer ... this writing is your answer to world outreach.

Combining real world military operations with the mandate from the Commander ... **you will find the keys for successful evangelization** of every tribe, language group, culture and nation. (Revelation 5:9)

Specific rules of engagement, guidelines and elements of war—with suggestions for options—are interspersed throughout the book at appropriate sections for **creative reflection and planning.**

How to implement the offensive—along with "What if's"—help the Christian worker to formulate a flexible, but systematic, plan of action. And, just as important, a methodized program for follow up **with maximum results**.

This book is more than a treatise on End Time evangelism. It is—at the same time—a construct for organic synthesis **to plant and grow new Messianic Synagogues and Churches**.

Act on your thoughts and instincts. **Lift up your vision.** Finish the work you've been assigned. The Mashiach of Israel is waiting!

The Art of Christian Warfare

■ ■ ■

Rules of Command

THE ART AND PRINCIPLES
OF CHRISTIAN WARFARE

Part of this book, *The Art of Christian Warfare,* was written in Africa and in the Republic of Mauritius by Prince Handley. It includes such topics as:

- Stratagem and tricks of the enemy.

- Guidelines for interactive ministry.

- How to operate in foreign cultures and countries.

- Secret powerful truths of ministry.

- When and how to work alone.

- When and how to work cooperatively.

- How to reach whole nations by yourself.

- Warrior mentality and diversionary tactics.

- Plus many other specifics of Christian warfare.

STRATAGEM AND TRICKS OF THE ENEMY

There are several strategies, tricks, and diversionary tactics of the enemy to halt, hinder, impede, nullify or destroy your ministry.

You must always be cognizant of this fact. There is a devil who has planned stratagem, and who has forces (spirits) of intelligence monitoring your plans, your progress, and your private relationships.

Do NOT be afraid. We will instruct you as to how to obtain and maintain the victory ... continually!

However, you need to be aware of the various stratagem of the devil. My purpose in writing this is so that you will be able to recognize his various tricks. If you know ahead of time how he works, then you will be able to resist and FIGHT as a strong warrior.

It is important in warfare to KNOW your enemy ... and to know HOW the tactical aspects of his warfare. Below are listed several methods of attack used by Satan. Some of his methods are:

➳ To get you to quit.

➳ To get you to cancel an engagement or speaking / teaching. Ways the enemy uses to get you to do this are as follows:

> Someone near you [associate, team member, driver--or family member of the same--"hanger-on," mixed multitude, etc.] is doubting, scoffing, heady [education versus the anointing] or high-minded.

> Someone you're teamed with is not being honest with you, or being "sneaky" and using you.

> Other speakers of different doctrine scheduled in the same meetings with you.

> Being hurt emotionally, spiritually, or physically. (See #5 below.)

➳ Diversionary tactics.

> Having you meet an attractive member of the opposite sex (single or married).

Opportunity(s) to make lots of money, or "quick money."

"Quick roads" to ministry success.

Fame: going for "your" name and NOT Jesus' glory. (See #4 below.)

➤ Pride

People not treating you right, or, respectfully ... and you may feel that you deserve better treatment (which you may).

Living a lifestyle for "show" or above your means.

CAUTION!
PRIDE IS A PSYCHOLOGICAL
ATTEMPT TO HIDE OUR FAULTS

➤ Emotional disappointment(s), "broken heart," or very rude action(s) on the part of others.

➤ Prolonged goal attainment or unaccomplished desire(s). Many times when we experience the "death of a vision" God brings resurrection; however, if a person is NOT persevering in faith, discouragement can set in.

➤ Death of a loved one.

➤ Lies, false accusations (or, true ones), gossip.

Not being used, included, or recognized. Being "shut out" by your peers or others, either purposefully or unknowingly.

Another person, or people, being promoted or recognized and you know they are NOT worthy of the recognition.

Sickness. You must claim and receive your healing. Go in faith unless the LORD tells you to stay.

A combination of any of the above.

POINTS TO REMEMBER

Walk DAILY in faith, pray in the Spirit, stay in the Word, obey the LORD, and keep your heart in forgiveness with love.

The Holy Spirit will always be leading you in the OPPOSITE direction of the devil.

The Holy Angels are assigned from God to protect you.

There are many promises in God's Word to give you victory.

Do NOT be afraid. Fear immobilizes the Body of Christ. Remember the old saying: *"Fear knocked at the door, faith answered, and no one was there!"* Speak this scripture to yourself often, *"For I have not received a spirit of fear, but of power, and love, and a sound mind (or, self control)."* (2 Timothy 1:7)

NOTES ON CHRISTIAN WARFARE

"And it came to pass, after the year was expired, at the time when the kings went to battle, that David sent Joab, and his servants with him, and all Israel; and they destroyed the children of Ammon, and besieged Rabbah. But David tarried still at Jerusalem." [2 Samuel 11:1]

David's GREATEST MISTAKE in life was staying behind at the time of year when other kings went to battle! Someone reading this today needs to hear this message! After many victories and much tribulation, at the peak of his career, David let his guard down! Don't you do it! The Spirit of God is having me give you this message TODAY!

Sylvester Stallone, in the movie *Rambo* does NOT accurately represent the real "Green Beret" soldier. The real "Green Berets" work together. And so should the Christian warriors!

NOTE #1: Know the real war, the real "warrior battle," or else the false battle will be upon you!

NOTE #2: The enemy wants you to think, *"I'm too old . . . the battle is for the young guys."* If you think this way, you'll become a casualty!

NOTE #3: It is not enough to defeat the enemy, you must occupy his territory!

NOTE #4: When there's strife at home, at work, in ministry, wherever, it's not the other person--IT'S THE ENEMY. Attack the enemy! *"Be wise as a serpent and harmless as a dove."*

NOTE #5: Always be a warrior . . . at all times!

NOTE #6: Media diversion (TV, DVD's, movies, and games), aimless travel, and the cares of this world are all "escape" from real combat. "R and R" (rest and recreation) is fine when needed but NOT for protracted periods of time, at least for the front lines warrior.

NOTE #7: What would a "warrior" lifestyle look like?

    Always in fellowship with other warriors.

    Disciplined (in all aspects).

    Anger against the enemy (from God) mixed with compassion for the oppressed.

    Doesn't play while his unit is in battle.

    Soldiers facing death (small group within a unit) will fight for each other out of loyalty to each other more than because of loyalty to superior officers.

LOOK FOR ANOTHER WARRIOR TO HELP

"For though we walk in the flesh, we do not war after the flesh (for the weapons of our warfare are not

fleshly, but mighty through God to the pulling down of strongholds); Casting down imaginations, and every high thing that exalts itself against the knowledge of God, and bringing into captivity every thought to the obedience of Christ."

"Finally, my brethren, be strong in the LORD, and in the power of his might. Put on the whole armor of God, that you may be able to stand against the wiles of the devil."

STRATEGIES OF THE ENEMY TODAY

Concerning David's sin with Bathsheba discussed previously, we see a double problem: [2 Corinthians 10:3-5] [Ephesians 6:10-11]

> He was resting when it was the regular time for kings to go to battle; and,

> He lusted after Bathsheba.

This double problem ended up in both adultery and murder, and brought much pain and unnecessary defeat into his life--and family--and kingdom. Had he gone to battle, the problem would probably never have started in the first place. The Bible tells, *"Commit your works unto the Lord, and your thoughts will be established."* [Proverb 16:3]

Concerning item #2, the lust after Bathsheba, I am including the section below to help you titled, ***"The Lust of the Eyes."***

The Lust of the Eyes - by Minister Davenport

One of the more sobering words for us is that with reference to "the lust of the eyes" (1 John 2:16); a fierce element of the larger spiritual battle currently being waged against us. This attack is year by year, and in a measure that is unprecedented. Those presently grappling with this stronghold, if left unchecked, may very soon be overcome by such, to the degree that they will **not** be able to control their eyes in public, and will thus be exposed.

A sobering warning should be issued, that those struggling with this issue should judge themselves privately, lest the Lord judge them (expose them) publicly. We are in the midst of a short season of grace wherein the Lord is calling His sheep to repent and breakaway from this stronghold. Prophetic and intercessory ministers are the figurative eyes of the Body of Christ. **It is therefore no surprise that those attacked most frequently by this force are often those called to move in the greatest measures of the prophetic and intercessory ministries**.

It is my belief therefore, that these attacks are an indirect affirmation of your call to the prophetic and/or intercessory ministry. It makes perfect sense therefore, that **if a Believer's vision is clouded and obscured with dark images, one's prophetic insight will therefore be clouded as well**. In essence, we are dealing with a "smoke screen" tactic from our adversary.

One of the most effective means by which one may rid themselves of this stronghold is that by way of confiding in another brother or sister, and acting upon

James 5:16, which reads: *"Confess your trespasses to one another, and pray for one another, that you may be healed."* This humble act releases the Sword of The Lord, to swiftly sever the chords of entanglement, and set free those who are captive. Remember that "...two can set 10,000 to flight...," for there is exponential power released when we band together to bring darkness into the light. When we do so, *"He shall deliver you from the snare of the fowler and from the perilous pestilence. He shall cover you with His feathers, and under His wings you shall take refuge;"* Ps. 91:3-4).

In addition to confiding and confession, **a specific fast for deliverance from this force can prove very effective**. During such a fast, a prayerful focus upon Psalm 25:15 delivers a powerful blow to this force. The verse reads as follows: *"My eyes are ever toward the Lord, for He shall pluck my feet out of the net."* With this verse as a prayer-platform, **one may pray literally, that the Lord keep their eyes "ever before Him,"** and thus find their feet being "plucked from the net" of the lust of the eyes.

If you have found yourself struggling with this issue, or know of others who are wrestling with the same, I encourage you to implement this prayer and fasting model, and pass it on to others as well.

NOTE BY PRINCE HANDLEY

Current surveys show that somewhere between 20% and 40% of pastors have a problem with pornography.

14

Depending upon the survey(s) it is a high percentage either way. I would tend to think that the higher percentage may be nominal pastors that may NOT be born again. This is one reason I included *"The Lust of the Eyes"* in part of Section 2. You need to counsel and help those under your watchcare; I was just asked by a long time friend and fellow minister to pray for him because of the problem he had with pornography.

Those in your watch care may be embarrassed to come foreward for help. Ask God to give you wisdom as to how to approach them for their deliverance. I might also suggest that you read (or listen to) a teaching I did titled: *Self Deliverance.* You may access in the Archives at: www.apostle.libsyn.com, September 21, 2009. If you will teach on that subject it may help someone who desires to remain anonymous about such a problem, but will them be able to take advantage of this method of deliverance.

WORD OF KNOWLEDGE

I am cognizant that while I am writing this there is someone who is participating in this scenario. God loves you! It is time for you to STOP. Go forward in a separated life so God can use you in SPECIAL works.

ASSIGNMENT

SHARE THIS MESSAGE WITH THREE (3) OTHER MINISTERS AND THREE (3) LAY PEOPLE

TEACH THIS MESSAGE EVERY THREE (3) MONTHS BY SOME MEANS: PUBLISHING, DIRECT MINISTRY, EMAIL, ETC.

THIS IS A SERIOUS PROBLEM FOR CHRISTIAN WOMEN, AS WELL AS MEN.

EXTRA STUDY RESOURCES:

IDEAS OF FAITH AND HOW TO GET RID OF FEAR

Read and prayerfully study *"Ideas of Faith: Acting on Your Thoughts,"* and *"How to Get Rid of Fear,"* included below. These two are included to protect from the stratagem of the enemy: Mental Attacks and Fear.

IDEAS OF FAITH: ACTING ON YOUR THOUGHTS

What I want to teach you about **"Ideas of Faith"** is probably something you have never received instruction concerning. Especially as a Christian . . . with ROYAL bloodline and ROYAL objectives . . . you need to "hit the mark." You need to have superior guidance so that you will effectively and efficiently accomplish the goals which your Father, the King of the Universe, has assigned to you. You have a job to do

16

that is unique. **No one has the same job classification in the Kingdom of God as you do**. You need to appropriate the data and information that is provided to you by the "Intelligence Sector" of the ROYAL Headquarters: Heaven.

If your know Jesus, the Messiah, personally, you are a child of the King. God has made you a citizen of a ROYAL nation and positioned you in the capacity of a priest. You are a priest TO GOD for people on earth, and you are a priest TO PEOPLE on Planet Earth for God, the Creator and Sustainer of the universe. **God has many ways to aid you** in the realm of intelligence and direction.

- His Word, the Holy Bible

- His Holy Spirit

- Gifts of the Holy Spirit

- Ministry of the Holy Angels

- Prophecy

- Providence and circumstantial experience

- Thoughts and instinct

Many times God is trying to lead you by means of your thoughts or instinct. For a Christian who has been baptized in the Holy Spirit, there are several gifts available to you: nine of which are listed in 1 Corinthians Chapter 12:8-11. Three categories of gifts:

POWER GIFTS

- Faith

- Working of miracles

- Healing

VOCAL GIFTS

- Tongues

- Interpretation of tongues

- Prophecy

WISDOM GIFTS

- Word of wisdom

- Word of knowledge

- Discerning of spirits

In context, the verses immediately before and after the listing of these nine gifts tell us **why, by Whom, and in what manner** these gifts are distributed.

Verse 7: *"But the manifestation of the Spirit is given to every man to profit."*

[Apostle Handley's note: *"For the contribution and good, for the profitableness of the individual and collectively for the Body of Christ."*]

Verse 11: *"But all these works that one and selfsame Spirit, dividing to every man severally as he will."*

Editor's note: "The Holy Spirit distributes each of the gifts upon and through each member separately as He wills."

There may be more than nine gifts of the Spirit; I would hate to think that the Spirit has limited Himself in creativity and benevolence and operation, especially for the good of His people. To study more about the Gifts of the Holy Spirit, read the book, *How to Receive God's Power with Gifts of the Spirit,* by Prince Handley (available on Amazon and at other fine book stores). It is plain to see that the three WISDOM GIFTS mentioned above provide ample insight into:

 Situations (word of knowledge);

 Actions to be taken (word of wisdom); and,

 Intelligence as to whether the situation has its origin from God or Satan! And so it is with **thoughts**--discerning of spirits.

Our Father, the God of Israel, instructs us as to the kind of thoughts we should be generating. Notice, we are able to GENERATE thoughts of a quality nature. *"Finally, brethren, whatsoever things are true, whatsoever things are honest, whatsoever things are just, whatsoever things are pure, whatsoever things are lovely, whatsoever things are of good report; if there be any virtue, and if there be any praise, think on these things."* [Philippians 4:8]

Notice, we can selectively either ACCEPT or REJECT thoughts based upon our "filter" of prerequisites! *"For though we walk in the flesh, we do not war after the flesh: For the weapons of our warfare are not carnal, but mighty through God to the pulling down of strongholds; Casting down imaginations, and every high thing that exalts itself against the knowledge of God, and bringing into captivity every thought to the obedience of Christ."* [2 Corinthians 10:3-5]

How many times have you had a thought that played out? Maybe it was something good that you really wanted . . . or maybe it was something you were afraid of. While in the process of writing this newsletter, I was talking to a person on the telephone who was not a Christian and who (not knowing I was writing on this subject) said to me, *"Whenever I have a thought about something it happens to me."*

The gifts of the Spirit work through LOVE. Galatians 5:6 tells us: *"For in Jesus Christ neither circumcision avails anything, nor uncircumcision; but faith which works by love."* **You can operate in faith if you use love, not fear!** But, you can't operate in faith if you use fear! There is an old saying, *"Fear knocked at the door; faith answered and no one was there."* And so it is with your thoughts and ideas, also. You need to make your thoughts and ideas work via the channel of love. Now, there are some thoughts which are neither based upon love or fear; they may be, for example, thoughts of folly.

For example, one day while writing, the LORD revealed a marvelous truth to me that He wanted me to share with His people in a teaching. I instantly had this thought: *"Lord, where do you come up with this stuff?!"* And then I laughed and asked God to forgive me. The revelation was so fantastic that I was amazed and was trying to pay God a compliment, forgetting for a moment that He is God and knows everything. I actually spent a few moments laughing (I'm sure with God) at my stupidity!

Here is a SECRET to great creativity. Ideas are a medium, a conduit: a channel for fear or faith. You have to "control" the pipeline! You will study in a later section on *"Choice of Warriors"* the subject **"Spirit-filled Control"** in the teaching by Prince Handley titled, *"Keys to Foundational Relationships."* **You have to "shut off" the ideas of fear and replace them with IDEAS OF FAITH. When you have thoughts of fear, replace them with VISUAL THOUGHTS.** By visualizing your thoughts; you can even add emphasis (power and potency) to them by decreeing them.

There is an amazing spiritual truth we find in Genesis 11:1-9. Before the nations of the earth were scattered on the face of the earth, the earth was of one language and one speech. The people had decided to make a city and a tower, whose top would reach unto heaven; they wanted to make a name for themselves so they would not be scattered abroad upon the face of the earth. *"And the Lord said, 'Behold, the people is one, and they all have one language; and this they begin to do: and now nothing will be restrained from them, which they have imagined to do."* [verse 6] *"Let us go down, and there confound their language, that they may not understand one another's speech."* [verse 7]

Archaeological records show us that these were wicked and idolatrous people. Yet we see in verse 6 that God said, *"nothing will be restrained from them."* **Notice they had ONE goal and ONE speech**. They were unified in purpose and language. If this principle of "oneness" works in unbelievers ... for ungodly, wicked people ... **how much more will it work for believers**

... for God's people ... who have ONE goal and ONE speech: a common vision and a common language! Especially spirit-filled Christians who have a common objective and who can pray and decree a thing (or a set of objectives) in not only their common earthly language(s), but also their heavenly language: tongues!

➡ In Job 22:28 we read, *"You shall also decree a thing, and it shall be established unto you ..."* In the original Hebrew language the word **"decree"** is a primitive root form of the word **"gazar"**, which means **"to cut out exclusively, or to decide"**. In its primitive form it is used also as a "quarrying" term ... as in cutting out stone from a rock quarry. It means more than to "say" or "speak". **It conveys the meaning of "cutting something out in your mind's eye"; that is, "to envision [to make a vision], to decide upon it, and confess it" ... and then it will be established unto you!** If you and your Christian brothers and sisters have a common vision or goal, and decide upon it, confessing it in a common language, speaking it ... **nothing will be restrained from you which you have imagined (or, envisioned) to do!** [Read again Genesis 11:1-6.]

IMPORTANT

USE VISUAL THOUGHTS WHEN YOU HAVE THOUGHTS OF CONCERN.

YOU WILL ELIMINATE MOST OF THE DEVIL'S ATTACKS ON YOUR MIND.

YOU WILL ALSO DESTROY SATANIC ACTIVITY IN ITS TRACKS!

➡ **So when you have thoughts of fear . . . about your family, your possessions, your health, your ministry . . . replace them with VISUAL THOUGHTS.** See the Holy Angels ministering to, blessing and guarding your family, your possessions, your health, and your ministry. See yourself (use a visual thought) with GREAT FAVOR being bestowed upon you. God promised you favor; why not appropriate it with IDEAS OF FAITH!

HOW TO GET RID OF FEAR

There are several types of fear. Fear of:

- Failure
- Broken relationships
- Not having enough
- Heights
- Disease
- People

- Success

- Not being mature

- Crowded areas

- Animals and creatures

- Enclosure

The Bible tells us *"For God has not given us the spirit of fear; but of power, and of love, and of a sound mind."* [2 Timothy 1:7] The Greek word for **"fear"** in the passage above is **"delia"** which means **"timidity."** The word for **"power"** is **"dunamis"** meaning **"miraculous power"** **implying a MIRACLE itself**. The word for **"love"** is **"agape"** meaning **"love or benevolence."** **"Sophronismos,"** the Greek word for **"sound mind"** actually means **"discipline or self control."** So, *God has NOT given us timidity, but He has given us a MIRACLE anointing, benevolent love, and self control*. We just need to KNOW this truth and in FAITH appropriate it in time of need. Pray this scripture . . . believe it . . . confess it.

Fear is a spirit; therefore, you must speak to it. God is love and He is spirit. Love is stronger than fear. Perfect love casts out fear. *"There is no fear in love; but perfect love casts out fear: because fear has torment. He that fears is not made perfect in love."* [1 John 4:18] **If you are afraid of someone, ask God to give you His love for them**. You can bind fear in the name of Jesus, and cast it away from you. Command it to leave, and use the name of Jesus against it. Speak (declare) the BLOOD of Christ against it. It is your responsibility to overcome fear.

SERIOUS cases of fear require four (4) steps:

    ☞ A stayed (fixed) mind. (You are NOT going to quit until you have total deliverance.)

    ☞ Confession of God's Word [1 John 4:18; James 4:7; 2 Timothy 1:7].

    ☞ A step of faith . . . action. Speak to fear and take authority over it.

    ☞ Intercession and spiritual warfare (for others or one's self).

Someone you know probably needs this message NOW. Think of someone you know who has had a repeated problem of fear over a long period of time---or shorter, since having been born again---but has NOT received freedom from, or over, their problem. The content of this section may be the answer for them; however, there are CONDITIONS that apply:

    ☞ They must be a born again believer;

    ☞ They must believe in **The Deliverer, Jesus**: in His POWER and WILLINGNESS to deliver them;

    ☞ They must know how to deliver others (even if they never have); and,

    ☞ They must really want deliverance. If a person knows Jesus Christ as their Lord, NO demon, NO evil spirit can have them! Jesus said, *"If the*

Son therefore shall make you free, you shall be free indeed." The Greek word here used for **"indeed"** [ontos] means **"really, actually."**

A great source for instruction on deliverance is the book, ***Healing Deliverance*** by Prince Handley. It is available on Amazon and at other fine book stores.

A person can minister **SELF deliverance** in most cases, even serious ones. Other than the Lord Jesus Christ, WHAT PERSON can pray for someone with such compassion and determination - and intimate knowledge of the problem(s) involved - than one's self?

Freedom from fear places people in a position of POWER and LOVE where they will experience a MIRACLE anointing and disciplined self control: the attributes which God has provided for us and which we receive by FAITH like any other gifts from the Father!

PRINCIPLES OF ENGAGEMENT
PRINCIPLE 1

GIVEN FACTS OF THE ENGAGEMENT

- Field: The world.

- Enemy: Satan.

- Mission: The mandate and directive of Christ.

WEAPONRY

- The Word of God

- The Holy Spirit

- The Name of Jesus

- The Blood of Christ

- The intercession of direction

SOME SIGNS OF ADVANCE IN RECENT YEARS

- Translation, publishing, and distribution of the Gospel in many modern languages.

- Intercession and prayer meetings for support

- Internet, iPhones, social media - Third Platform.

- New ideas of missions--leaders listening to the Spirit.

MILITARY TACTICS TO BE USED BY PRAYER AND EVANGELISTIC FORCES

When I was a little boy, on about every block in the city, someone's relative had either lost their life or been wounded fighting for freedom on both sides of our world; and usually to help people in other countries be free. I lost my brother and my cousin. My brother won two Silver Stars, four Bronze Stars, two Purple Hearts, and several other medals.

My brother helped saved many men on a burning amphibian. Another time, he willingly gave his life to save his men. A sniper was hidden in a tree shooting at them with a machine gun and they could not detect where he was at. My brother, a lieutenant, ran out to purposely draw the enemy's fire so they could detect where he was at. The sniper cut my brother in to pieces with his machine gun fire; however, it saved the lives of his men.

We too, as Christian soldiers, must be prepared to give our lives. Our Master is the supreme example! We are in a war! The purpose of this study series is to teach you the ART and PRINCIPLES of warfare so that you can transfer these principles to the spiritual war in which you are involved. Particularly, you will learn how to employ EVANGELISM and PRAYER in combat so that you can effectively take villages and communities, cities, regions, nations, and continents for Christ.

The first thing you must do is study--and re-study-- Prince Handley's booklet entitled, *How To Win The World For Christ.* There are seven (7) keys in it which will assure your success. Jesus was NOT paranoid; neither was He schizophrenic. He commanded us to *"Go into all the world and preach the gospel to every creature."* You will see how easy this job is to do in this booklet. [You will find this material later in "Principles of Engagement - Principle #7.]

➡ Admiral Nimitz, a great Admiral in the U.S. Navy during World War II, in a handwritten letter to his sister, Mary Aquinas, a Catholic nun, said that there are **three (3) elements of successful war:**

    ✏ Offensive;

- Surprise; and,

- Autonomy of force (freedom of action; not having to check with someone over you).

As far as the ART and PRINCIPLES of war, here are some rules laid down by master militarists through the ages. Learn these principles and then transfer them into your combat for the Lord. Effective use of these principles will guarantee your victory; to disregard them will set you up for defeat.

PRINCIPLES OF ENGAGEMENT

PRINCIPLE #1 - THE OFFENSIVE

The only time you do a "fighting withdrawal" is for the purpose of DELAY in order to buy time for:

- More troops, and/or

- More equipment.

Short supply lines are to your advantage; don't be too far ... or in a position where it takes too much time to receive supplies: literature, food, workers, equipment.

Train the way you fight, and fight the way you train.

Study Joshua 1:1-8. God gives his warriors strategy. You must PRAY and LISTEN. He also gives protection, victory, and MIRACLES!

The Supreme Commander, Jesus Christ, has assigned the overall objective:

> "All power is given to me in heaven and in earth. You go, therefore, and teach all nations." [Matthew 28:15]

Sun Tzu, who wrote *The Art of War* in 500 B.C. said, "In war then, let your great object be victory, not lengthy campaigns."

Choose an objective that is not so distant that it is UNobtainable. The objective is the most important.

"They want war too methodical, too measured; I would make it brisk, bold, impetuous, perhaps sometimes even audacious." [Jomini: *Jomini's Art of War*, written by Lt. Colonel J. D. Hittle]

Be on the OFFENSIVE
Be the AGGRESSOR
Win the ADVANTAGE

You make the decisions **before** the enemy.

➡ **The enemy has to wait to find out** WHERE you are going to attack, WHEN you are going to attack and WHAT you are going to do.

The above are KEY elements in **evangelism strategy**.

The OFFENSIVE must be **planned strategically**, and **directed specifically**.

➤ Against a broad area or front line of the enemy: a country or region; or,

Against one KEY VITAL POINT, the fall or capture of which, would produce a strategic break which would weaken the enemy's forces, or produce defeat for the enemy.

Missiles and air bombardment, carried out for several weeks or months, can weaken the enemy substantially before ground forces attack. So with prayer and concentrated intercession for the objective, the forces--the preachers and Christian workers--the confusion of the enemy will be effected before the workers of Christ attack in witness, preaching, and ministry.

The offensive is conducted through:

Preaching, and

Prayer

Discern WHAT or WHERE is the KEY VITAL POINT of the enemy's territory.

QUESTIONS

WHAT IS A "KEY VITAL POINT" IN YOUR NEXT OBJECTIVE?

WHERE IS A "KEY VITAL POINT" IN YOUR NEXT OBJECTIVE?

By taking this KEY VITAL POINT (that is, by winning a decisive victory there) you may then use the PRINCIPLES of war **from that KEY VITAL POINT**.

To determine the KEY VITAL POINT, two conditions must be met:

Relative importance to the whole; and,

Practicability of capture (it can be done successfully).

The offense must be:

Bold,

Toward the enemy (advance),

Make use of effective weapons. You must have intercession and praying in the Spirit as "air support" to back up the preachers and ministers.

The offensive is directed against the enemy (Satan) ... not the objective (the area of attack).

After the decisive attack on the KEY VITAL POINT is successful, you must then **OCCUPY THE LAND ...** and announce to those Satan has held in bondage that **they are FREE**. Set them free.

Start Bible studies.

Start house churches. Build network(s) of same.

Start community healing and deliverance rooms.

NOTE: For Bible Studies and Rabbinical Studies, go to www.marketplaceworld.com. Select "Study Materials." **You can access all of the following FREE:**

- French Bible Studies

- Spanish Bible Studies

- English Bible Studies

- Rabbinical Studies

▶ **Build disciples!!!** (Many people have received MIRACLES while studying the materials above.)

There are five (5) players on the field:

1. God,

2. God's servant(s),

3. The Holy Angels,

4. Satan (plus a 6th player: demons). However, when you bind the "strong man"—Satan--then you will subjugate his demons.

5. The occupants (the people that Satan has bound).

The objective is evangelizing people, cities, nations, continents. And, then occupying the territory previously held by the enemy by planting local groups of believers (synagogues or churches)--these may be underground or house groups--from which apostles and teachers will be raised up and then apostles sent out to start NEW bodies (groups) of believers for Messiah. (Read Acts 13:1-4.) Do you see the order of events and callings?: **1. Prophets and teachers raised up; then, 2. Apostles sent out.**

33

Move toward the objective preaching and praying!

PRINCIPLES OF ENGAGEMENT

PRINCIPLES #2 AND #3

PRINCIPLE 2 – CONCENTRATION

Jim Wilson, in his book *Principles of War* portrays a vivid example of the power of CONCENTRATION. In WW II a group of American fighter pilots known as the "*Flying Tigers*" were "*outnumbered in the air and on the ground, in planes, pilots, and parts,*" yet they "*destroyed 217 enemy planes and probably 43 more with a maximum of 20 operational P-40's [fighter planes] in 31 encounters.*" The Americans only lost 6 pilots and 16 planes. **This was accomplished by CONCENTRATION. They used TWO (2) airplanes firing at ONE (1) of the enemy!**

This is why Jesus sent His disciples out "**two and two**." "*After these things the Lord appointed other seventy also, and sent them two and two before his face into every city and place, where He himself would come.*" [Luke 10:1]

We see this same principle in prayer. "*Again I say unto you, that if two of you shall agree on earth as touching anything that they shall ask, it shall be done for them of my Father which is in heaven. For where two or three are gathered together in my name, there am I in the midst of them.*" [Matthew 18:19-20]

QUESTION

IN WHAT AREAS OF OFFENSIVE SHOULD YOU BE USING CONCENTRATION?

We have studied the two elements of OFFENSIVE and CONCENTRATION. In the offensive the objective is evangelizing people, cities, nations, continents through:

- Prayer, and

- Preaching

Jesus sent His workers out to PRAY and PREACH in CONCENTRATION!

PRINCIPLE 3 - CHOICE OF WARRIORS

Your choice of associates is probably one of the most important decisions you will ever make. It involves probably some long term associates as well as short term associates. In many cases it will involve your helpmate, or spouse.

The Bible teaches: *"A man that hath friends must show himself friendly: and there is a friend that sticks closer than a brother."* [Proverb 18:24]

I studied under four of the Greek and Hebrew scholars who worked on the translation of the *New American Standard Version* of the Bible. The American Standard Version of the above scripture renders it: *"He that maketh many friends [doeth it] to his own destruction; But there is a friend that sticketh closer than a brother."*

Also, the Greek manuscript, the *Syriac*, the *Targum* (an Aramaic paraphrase of the Old Testament), the *Vulgate* (an ancient translation of the Bible into Latin), and the *Masoretic Text* (the traditional Hebrew Old Testament) all render the verse as saying: *"He that makes many friends may come to ruin ..."*

In other words, you increase the odds of becoming vulnerable each time you add a new friend. With each new association (not even counting the possibilities of old relationships falling apart) you expose yourself to being attacked or harmed.

This may sound like a negative approach at the subject; however, my job is to make you aware of the importance of good relationships ... and especially **those decisions concerning your choice of warriors**. It is better to have NO friends at all and just be with Jesus - who sticks closer than a brother - than to be injured in battle by an associate ... even if it's "friendly fire."

Now, let's take the positive approach. We walk by faith, not by fear. We must pray for the right choice of associates. Especially the inner circle of associates. Sometime this association--or nucleus of associates--develops over a long period of time ... sometimes, instantly.

King David, who had gathered an amazing band of faithful warriors, had this to say:

"For it was nor an enemy that reproached me; then I could have borne it: neither was it he that hated me that did magnify himself against me; then I would have hid myself from him. But it was you, a man mine equal, my guide, and my acquaintance. We took sweet

counsel together, and walked unto the house of God in company." [Psalm 55:12]

Pray carefully about, not only your associates, but especially your choice of warriors: those with whom you go into battle. The war you are engaged in is more serious than any that has ever been fought in the whole history of the world. Don't take it lightly!

ITEMS TO CONSIDER
WHEN CHOOSING WARRIORS

- Is he or she a person of integrity?

- Are their children, if any, serving the Lord?

- Has this warrior been tested or proven in the field?

- How do I feel in my heart about this person? Any reservations?

First, start with the basic tools for foundational relationships: these apply to any and all relationships. I have now been ministering for 50 years. **Through these years I have discovered seven (7) "*Power Keys*" for successful relationships**. If you will adhere to these keys outlined below, you will have an unshakeable foundation for your life, your family, your ministry ... and the battle(s) before you.

KEY 1 - BE COMMITTED FIRST TO GOD.

This commitment starts with daily Bible reading and study. God will lead you in whatever commitments you need to make to, or with, people.

KEY 2 - GIVE POSITIVE SUPPORT TO THE ONES TO WHOM YOU COMMIT.

Tell the people you're committed to: "God will fight for us!" Criticize the devil ... NOT people!

KEY 3 - BE ENCOURAGED IN HOW GOD HAS WORKED THROUGH YOU, AND THROUGH OTHERS, IN THE PAST.

Forget disappointments: in people or events. Don't look back, except at the successes and the good.

KEY 4 - MAKE SURE YOU'RE IN CONTROL ... ALWAYS CONTROL:

- Thoughts;

- Activities ... have a plan! Remember to plan for recreation and rest;

- The devil; and,

- Associations.

KEY 5 – GIVE. HAVE FUN GIVING FOR A LIFE OF SERVICE.

Stay under the anointing by "giving out" to others in the name of Jesus. As you minister to others, you will be ministered to! Look for needs to meet: people who need healing; people who need help, counsel, or prayer ... and then meet the need.

As you pray for others, or help them or minister to them, you will between them and God. You will be "under the anointing." As you pray for the sick, Christ's healing power will flow through you. As you encourage others, you will be encouraged. Also, "You will reap what you sow." As you give to the poor, God will give back to you!

KEY 6 - BE RESPONSIBLE - HAVE A BASE OF OPERATIONS.

Always have a place where people can contact you: where the LIFE of Christ can flow through you to help them or to follow up with them ... you want them to GROW and become POWERFUL and PRODUCTIVE in Christ!

KEY 7 - PRAY IN THE SPIRIT'S LANGUAGE AND IN YOUR LANGUAGE.

Build yourself up continually in your relationships with God and with people by praying! Start and continue your day praying in tongues and in your language. Let the Holy Spirit build you up and, also, pray intelligently in matters for which you don't know what to pray. See Jude 20 and Romans 8:26-27.

SUMMARY OF THE SEVEN KEYS

You need to have strong relationships with God and with those people with which God will lead you to work. Appreciate the people with which God has chosen you to work. However, don't try to "force" relationships: don't make commitments to every person you meet. God will show you those people to whom you should be committed when you are FIRST committed to Him!

Give positive support, or "reinforcement" to those people to whom you have committed ... whether:

> ☞ They are OVER YOU in a position of authority;

> ☞ You are OVER THEM; or,

> ☞ You are on the same level (working or ministry associates).

Remind each other that "God will fight for us!" Give your associates REWARDS from time-to-time for:

> ☞ The good work they do;

> ☞ Their consistency and faithfulness; or,

> ☞ Their availability.

These rewards do not (always) have to be monetary. **Sometimes a "pat on the back," or a "word of encouragement," is really meaningful**: letting them know the good they are doing is not going unnoticed. Let people KNOW you are THANKFUL and APPRECIATIVE of their association with you. Maybe an invitation to dinner, or just spending time alone with them or their family, whether it's a few minutes or a day or two.

It is also important for a man to give positive support to his wife. There are so many ways a wife serves a husband in his ministry that may go unnoticed by him. We need to appreciate those nearest to us, and never to take them for granted. This is where "family altar" is so important: don't neglect ministering to your own family! They may be your GREATEST DISCIPLES!! Read and discuss the Holy Bible together, and then pray together.

It is good to spend time refreshing your mind thinking about all the successes God has given you in the past. **God has NOT brought you this far to make you fail.** God is FOR you! One time the disciples of Jesus were in a ship in the middle of the sea where the waves were rough and the wind was strong. They became fearful until Jesus came to them walking on the water. He told them not to be afraid. They FORGOT that the Lord had commanded them to GO to the other side. He did NOT intend them to sink or to fail. **Jesus intends for you to SUCCEED! Jesus intends for YOU to make it to the other side!**

Take time to study in the Holy Bible how others have succeeded: Abraham, Joseph, Daniel, Esther, Mordecai and the Apostles. Study Prince Handley's *Militant Church History* and see how many other Christians have become successful in the Church. They were HUMAN just like you! **Don't meditate on past failures; it is a trick of the devil to form a "failure image" on your mind.** Forget past failures ... **don't look back, except at the SUCCESSES and the GOOD!** (Philippians 4:8.)

Looking back at past successes (and NOT looking back at past failures) is easy if you learn how to CONTROL YOUR THOUGHTS. Don't allow Satan to put bad images on your mind; and don't allow him to use the bad imaginations (image-thoughts) YOU can put on your mind.

"For though we walk in the flesh, we do not war after the flesh: (for the weapons of our warfare are not carnal, but mighty through God to the pulling down of strongholds); casting down imaginations [of your own and arguments of others], and every high thing that exalts itself against the knowledge of God, and bringing into captivity every though to the obedience of Christ." [2 Corinthians 10:3-5]

"Finally, brethren, whatsoever things are true, whatsoever things are honest, whatsoever things are just, whatsoever things are pure, whatsoever things are lovely, whatsoever things are of good report: if there be any virtue, and if there be any praise, think on these things." [Philippians 4:8]

To be a good steward you must be IN CONTROL of **the areas, domains, facilities, and personnel**:

☞ Over which God has placed you; and,

☞ Over which God has given you power and authority.

The reason you must exercise control is so that you may carry out the work God has given you to do. **You must do it the way God has told you to do it**. You must CONTROL not only your thoughts, but also your ACTIVITIES. Have a plan.

Know where you're headed: each day and in the future ... to the end of your life. You must be flexible and follow the leading of the Spirit. God may want you to change your plan(s) at times, but spend time alone with God so that you can hear from Him and establish your goals: both short-range and long-term (lifetime).

Each day when you arise (except your Sabbath day of rest) have a list already made out with the activities you

42

want to accomplish numbered in order of importance (or, priority). To help you do this, every night (or whenever you find convenient time---although forming the habit of making out your list at the same time every day is best---write down on a sheet of paper the "THINGS TO DO" or, "activities" for the next day.

After you have made your list, go back over it and assign numbers (starting with #1) to the most important thing, and then the things of lesser importance. Then, make out another list, writing down the activities in order of importance: #1, #2, #3, etc. You may not accomplish all the things you have written down for the day; however, you will have accomplished the MOST IMPORTANT things. Again, allow for flexibility: the Holy Spirit may change your plans the next day; or, you may find the next day that Item #4 on your list should be exchanged for a position of higher priority with, for example, Item #2.

You must CONTROL the devil, Satan. Jesus said, *"Behold, I give unto you POWER . . . over all the power of the enemy."* (Luke 10:19). Jesus gave you POWER:

Over the demons (see verse 20);

Over the power of the devil;

Over Satan, himself.

This is part of the **Covenant of Freedom** which Jesus Christ (the Anointed One, the Messiah of Israel) purchased for you with His own BLOOD! You are FREE: free from the devil, sin, and the world; and you are free to serve God! **YOU are FREE to be the person God has called you to be**!

43

In Matthew 12, verses 22-29, Jesus said, *"I cast out devils by the Spirit of God. How can one enter into a strong man's house [or, the devil's house], and spoil his goods, except he first BIND the strong man? And then he will spoil his [the devil's] house."* The binding and loosing power of the Church is one of the teachings of Jesus. Jesus said, *"Whatever you will bind on earth will be bound in heaven: and whatever you will loose on earth will be loosed in heaven."* (Matthew 18:18.)

Study, Prince Handley's teaching on **Binding and Loosing**. (Available online at *Apostle Talk: Future News Now!* Blog at **www.apostle.libsyn.com**. Go to Archives June 18, 2014.)

Finally, you must exercise control over your associations. This does not mean you have to control your associates; but rather, **be in control of the decision making process with regard to the person(s) with whom you will be associated** and those with whom you will NOT be associated.

Remember **KEY #1**, be committed first to God and then God will lead you in whatever commitments you need to make to, or with, people. There are some people with whom it would NOT be profitable in the Spirit for you to be closely associated. This does not mean you do not love them, nor that you do not communicate with them or even work together with them, at times, in the Lord's work. It does mean, however, that they are not your close associates.

One crucially important area to watch for is association with gossips. **Never associate closely with gossips**; never have them work for you. Love them and tell them about their sin. If a person gossips about other people, you can be sure that under the right circumstances that person will gossip about you!

By knowing this fact ahead of time and operating wisely you can save yourself (and the Lord's work) from much harm. Be well advised (or, forewarned) to stay away from busybodies, gossips, and slanderers. Especially, have no close association with them, except to minister to them and help them.

Jesus ministered to thousands. He also had eleven disciples He poured his life into (the twelfth one was a devil, preordained by the Scriptures). However, Jesus also had a very close relationship with an inner circle of three: Peter, James and John. God has given you the FREEDOM TO CHOOSE and He will also give you the LEADING TO KNOW with whom to be closely associated.

Don't try to have associates just to have associates. If God wants you to have some close associates He will cross your path with those of like mind and faith; those with whom you can:

⟶ Have wonderful fellowship;

⟶ Have common faith to believe God for great things;

⟶ Share personal needs, wants, or dreams (aspirations).

There may be times when God would have you (He will lead you by His Spirit) to dissolve relationships that are already established. You must be very careful to listen and obey God in these times or your ministry could suffer greatly.

When you dissolve a relationship with someone, it does not mean you do not love them, nor that you do not communicate with them (unless God is leading you NOT to communicate with them). Remember, the key is: Be committed first to God!

Be responsible. **Be available to help others in whatever way God leads you**. You may have to "sweat" and work hard. You may shed tears at times, but you will have the JOY of the LORD, and that will be your strength.

Serve God because you love Him and you're thankful for what He has done for you ... and for what He's doing for you even NOW that you MAY NOT SEE or know about ... and then thank Him for what He will do for you in the future! Pray--in your language and in tongues—and ask for only God's choice of associates.

PUT GOD FIRST AND GO FORWARD!

PRINCIPLES OF ENGAGEMENT
PRINCIPLES #4, #5, and #6

PRINCIPLE 4 - ENDURANCE & COURAGE

Napoleon Bonaparte said that the main priorities of a soldier are:

    Endurance of fatigue, and

✎ Courage.

In the *Book of Joshua*, we see that when God was giving instructions to Joshua about mounting the offensive to conquer the land on the other side of the Jordan River, He told him three (3) times *"Be strong and of a good courage,"* and then finally on the fourth occasion, *"Do not be afraid nor be dismayed, for the Lord your God is with you wherever you go."*

Do NOT be afraid. Fear immobilizes the Body of Christ. Remember the old saying: *"Fear knocked at the door, faith answered, and no one was there!"* **Speak this scripture to yourself often**, *"For I have not received a spirit of fear, but of power, and love, and a sound mind (or, self control)."* [2 Timothy 1:7]

In the T.A.S.E.R program [The Apostles School of Evangelistic Reform] we instruct people how to witness and minister working with the Holy Spirit.

Our Commander admonishes us as follows:

"Be ye strong therefore, and not your hands be weak: for your work shall be rewarded." [2 Chronicles 15:7]

"Therefore, my beloved brethren, be ye steadfast, unmovable, always abounding in the work of the Lord, forasmuch as you know that your labor is not in vain in the Lord." [1 Corinthians 15:58]

PRINCIPLE 5 - FREEDOM OF MOVEMENT

You cannot retreat or regroup if you are immobile; neither can you attack.

You must be able to move faster, farther, and function longer than your enemy in any offensive you plan . . . as well as the overall campaign.

➡ **IF NO OFFENSIVE IS PLANNED, FREEDOM OF MOVEMENT IS OF NO VALUE.**

If we retreat, it is only that we may regroup to attack either more wisely or with more power and concentration, or both.

You cannot mount an offense in concentration to strike a decisive blow at a place of your choosing unless you have freedom of movement.

Remember ... your offense is conducted with:

➤ Prayer, and

➤ Preaching.

You must have freedom of movement in BOTH of these areas.

CHECK THIS OUT

➤ Intercession gives greater distance, accuracy, speed and power.

➤ Intercession facilitates freedom of movement.

➤ What is your next offensive? What is next year's offensive?

Obtain a map of your country and of the world. Lay hands on the cities and nations and pray for God to:

48

↞ Send out the laborers;

↞ Pour out His spirit upon them;

↞ Raise up Bible schools in the areas; and,

↞ Raise up new, great Spirit baptized churches.

➡ Don't forget to "bind" the enemy. Then "loose" the activity you desire!

PRINCIPLE 6 - CHARACTER OF LEADERSHIP

The deeper your character . . . the greater your impact!

Many of the problems, challenges, and temptations that come your way are TESTS. God wants to SEE your response, and sometimes your reaction, to the test. **Are you worthy of Him investing more gifts and abilities in you?** Can He depend upon you - yes, and can people depend upon you - to be a good steward of what is placed under your control?

Ask yourself this question: **"Have I been a good steward over the things that God has given me by birth, assignment, or adoption?"** Every day you should plead—declare---the BLOD of Jesus over these, both now and in the future.

A leader not only is a good steward of these things, but he or she also has VISION. A leader meets needs:

↞ Orphans, the fatherless, the widows;

↞ Poverty;

✏ Aids / HIV and pandemic crises;

✏ Training of new leaders.

Leaders may not be the first ones to see the problem(s); but they are usually the first one to meet the needs. They have courage. Without courage, what should be AND could be, won't be!

Aristotle said, *"The soul never thinks without a picture."* Likewise, **a leader will have a vision of the God ordained task ahead**. Dream no small dreams! Study Prince Handley's companion books dealing with The Vision: *Action Keys for Success* and *How to Do Great Works*. (Available in e-Book and Paperback formats at Amazon and other book stores.)

We see the example of leadership modeled in the life of our Lord. The servant is not greater than his master, yet Jesus came "to serve ... not to be served." How many ministries today are using disciples to "serve" leadership under the guise of "covering."

A leader is an example in every area of life; **a triumphant Christian leader is a soul winner**.

A leader is also one who **"makes waves."** When a leader recognizes a need he or she will attempt to fix it even if the situation has to be confrontational. Pray . . . then go and do! It's not so much **IF** you rock the boat . . . but **HOW**! A leader challenges the status quo. A leader challenges the process.

Leadership is the God given ability to SEE leadership potential in everyone. Look at how Jesus saw this in the disciples. The careless became courageous. The foolish became faithful.

David learned to be a leader during the time he was alone as a shepherd. If he didn't learn how to fight off a lion and a bear he would have lost sheep. He learned to be a protector of the flock.

SUGGESTION

WRITE DOWN SOME WAYS TO

ENHANCE YOUR CHARACTER

THEN ACT!

PRINCIPLES OF ENGAGEMENT
PRINCIPLE #7

PRINCIPLE 7 - HOW TO WIN THE WORLD FOR MESSIAH YESHUA (JESUS)

I am going to teach you something that will help you win the world for Messiah Jesus!

If you could win 1,000 people to Messiah (Christ) every day, how long do you think it would take to evangelize the whole world? At this time, the population of the world is a little over seven (7) billion people. It would take you 19,726 years to reach every person (even at 1,000 every day!).

However, if you would lead only one person each year to Christ, and would really train them, here's what would happen: At the end of one year there would be two of you to take the "Good News" to others. If each of you would lead one person to Christ that next year, there would be four of you at the end of the second year to go tell the "Good News". At this rate, it would only take you **less than 23 years to reach the rest of the world!** (Even if the population increases to 8.4 billion, it would still only take 23 years.)

This is why Yeshua (Jesus) said, *"Go, then to all peoples of the world and make them my disciples: baptize them in the name of the Father, the Son, and the Holy Spirit, and teach them to obey everything I have commanded you. And remember! I will be with you always, to the end of the age."*

Now, here's how to train a disciple: **Ask God to lead you to someone who really wants to grow in the Lord** (it may be someone you lead to Christ or someone who already knows Jesus.) Take them "under your wing" (like a bird does her babies) and pour your life, as well as the Word of God, into them. You will have to "live" the life you are teaching about.

Take them preaching on the streets or witnessing at the market with you. Teach them how to lead others to Christ, and to baptize them in water. Their training may last from one week, or until Jesus comes back! Sometimes you may want to train more than one person at a time. However, never get so busy that you do not have time to spend with each person privately.

When a person you are training starts training others for Christ (it may be the first week), then spend some time for "feedback". That is, let that person discuss with you about the people they are training: get "feedback" about progress or problems, and try to answer their questions. Pray with them!

Be sure to tell the people you are teaching that Messiah Yeshua said, *"The field is the world!"* Not just their village or city: but every nation, tribe, tongue, and dialect. Pray that God will send out workers to the nations ... and be willing to go yourself. Teach them to do the same. **Obtain a map of the world** (and of your country). **Lay your hands on the different countries and cities and pray for them. Ask God:**

     To pour out the Holy Spirit on them,

     To send out Christian workers to them,

     To raise up "Spirit-filled" churches in them and all over the world.

While praying for cities and nations, always "**bind**" the devil and his demons and cast them out in Jesus' name. Then, "**loose**" the Holy Spirit into the cities and nations! Jesus said, *"Teach them to obey everything I have commanded you."* This includes his teaching about love, repentance, healing, forgiveness, casting out demons, prayer, baptism in the Holy Spirit, and our "one-ness" with other believers in Jesus.

Some of the people you train may be from other countries (students or visitors). Or, some of those you train may someday go to other countries to study, tour, or work. They will then be able to preach the Gospel there. This is another way you will be reaching nations!

Finally, teach the ones you are training to teach people they teach "**to teach others**." (Notice the four groups, or "families," of disciples in 2 Timothy 2:2.) The first family is YOU: you are a disciple, or a "follower," of Messiah Jesus. The next family is the person you are teaching to be a "follower" of Messiah. Notice something very important: the four families are NOT your disciples, they are Messiah's disciples!

The diagram below shows you the extreme importance of making "disciples" (not your disciples, but Christ's.) Now, YOU can win the world for Messiah Yeshua (Jesus)!

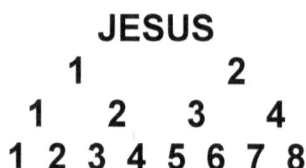

JESUS

1   2

1   2   3   4

1 2 3 4 5 6 7 8

NOTE: Read this message again, and again, and again. There are "seven keys" to help YOU win the world for Christ!

Now that you know **HOW** to win the world for Christ, make sure you have the **POWER** you need to do it! Study Prince Handley's book, *How to Receive God's Power with Gifts of the Spirit*. (Available at Amazon and other book stores.)

Also study, *New Global Strategy: Enabling Missions*, by Prince Handley. (Available at Amazon and other book stores.)

ASK GOD TO CROSS YOUR PATH WITH PEOPLE YOU CAN DISCIPLE

PRINCIPLES OF ENGAGEMENT
PRINCIPLE #8

PRINCIPLE 8 - SELF GOVERNING INDEPENDENCE

We discussed in "Military Tactics" under Principle 1, that during World War II, Admiral Nimitz, a great naval warrior, wrote a hand written letter to his sister, Sister Mary Aquinas, a Catholic nun. In that letter, Admiral Nimitz wrote that there are **three elements of successful war**:

- Offensive,

- Surprise, and

- Autonomy of force.

The definition of **autonomy** is **"self government; freedom of action."** A warrior's group, be it large or small, must have the liberty to exercise offensives of whatever kind when and where it feels necessary. Unless the leader of the group feels it is necessary, or for any other reason he or she feels obliged, **he should normally not have to check with the commander of the unit above** him unless it is for logistical reasons. [Logistics will be covered in Principle #14.]

It stands to reason, that when making a concerted offensive with other groups, communication is of primary importance so that the offensive is coordinated. **In that case, autonomy of force is dictated by the overall goal of all groups combined**.

➡ However, in an emergency, the individual group leaders have to operate with self governing independence.

In the Army of God, being directed by the Spirit in such decisions is mandatory. In the movies, "Rambo" is portrayed as an individual warrior; but in reality, the real Green Berets work together as a unit, no matter how small. But ... they are an autonomous unit, with freedom of action based upon the situation, the environment, and the time.

Do NOT be confined by having to check with a church committee or mission board in order to carry out an offensive you KNOW the Holy Spirit wants effected.

➡ Do NOT be confined by having to check with someone (or a group) that claims to be your "covering." This is a trick of the devil to kill the evangelistic and prophetic anointing, with the end result that NO real apostolic ministry is raised up.

In the Early Church we see that there were prophets and teachers. As they ministered to the Lord and fasted, the Holy Spirit said, *"Now separate to me Barnabas and Saul for the work to which I have called them."* Then having fasted and prayed, and laid hands on them, they sent them away. They became apostles (sent ones).

➡ This is the normal New Testament pattern. As new cell groups and Bible studies [in some cases, schools] are raised up, teaching and prophetic ministry arises. Then . . . **apostles are sent out to start new works, where the CYCLE then repeats in a self propagating living organism: the Body of Messiah.**

WARNING

↝ It is the objective of your enemy (Satan, the devil) to kill this cycle.

↝ The enemy may use Christian leaders to attempt this.

↝ The enemy will try to use infiltration of ministry, false teaching and maybe false covering (making disciples of men and NOT of Christ) to interrupt this cycle.

↝ The **BLOOD** of Christ is your covering!

Most of the people in the false covering or false discipleship movement (the "shepherding" movement) have never been in the trenches of real Christian warfare: open air evangelism and soul winning. They prey on converts of others. Many are good teachers, but **their teaching is camouflaged and deadly to REAL apostolic ministry and long term organic church growth.**

PRINCIPLES OF ENGAGEMENT
PRINCIPLE #9

PRINCIPLE 9 - SECURITY AND INTELLIGENCE

To be secure, you must know what the enemy is doing and, as much as possible, what he is planning AND you must provide protection for your group. You must have knowledge of the enemy's communications AND protect your communications from being "hacked" or intercepted. Know what the enemy is doing and planning, but don't let the enemy know what you're doing and planning. You must have trustworthy intelligence . . . and trustworthy associates.

I have a "war room" where I live. No one is allowed there. (Only two people, other than myself, have been there: a maid who cleans for me and a granddaughter I was taking care of.) It is where I have meticulous and detailed plans of projects for offensives in the Spirit. It is where I listen to the Holy Spirit and receive instructions from my Supreme Commander, the Messiah of Israel. I post large 27 X 34 inch (69 X 86 cm) project plans on my walls; I have binders for each major project with detailed work plans and strategies; I have a large map of the world, and I listen constantly to international news.

In this "war room" I listen to the Holy Spirit. First, I seek His direction as to WHAT offensives I am to conduct . . . then HOW, WHEN, and WITH WHOM I am to initiate them. You are reading this material right now that was initiated in the "war room" nine years ago.

Satan is limited in his knowledge, whereas God is omniscient. God knows everything, but Satan does not. God is omnipotent: He is all powerful, but Satan is limited in power ... and we have God's power available to us in several types of weaponry:

- The name of Jesus,

- The Blood of Christ,

- The Word of God,

- The shield of faith,

- The Holy spirit

- The tongues (praying in the Spirit),

- The Holy Angels

- The holy life.

In 2 Corinthians 2:11, the Apostle Paul told us not to be ignorant of the devil's devices lest he should get an advantage of us. We have superior power and weaponry over the enemy, but **we must establish intelligence (knowledge of how the enemy operates) and security (setting up defense)**. We have been given a "field manual" for defense, Ephesians 6:10-18, the whole armor of God. Armor is used for BOTH offense and defense.

QUESTIONS

- Is there a weak place in your armor inviting attack from Satan or his agents (human or other)?

- What offensive can you implement to take new ground for the Lord and to advance the Kingdom?

Why should Satan attack us where we are strong? He will look for the weak points: the points where his forces can slip through ... or break through. That's why "the holy life" is listed as weaponry above. The Bible instructs us: *"Neither give **place** to the devil."* [Ephesians 4:27] The word "place" here used in the Greek is "topos" and is a military term. **We are to give no location or opportunity for the enemy to attack us**. In the book, *The Art of War*, Sun Tzu said:

> *"The good fighters of old first put themselves beyond the possibility of defeat ... and then ...*
>
> *"Waited for an opportunity to defeat the enemy."*

God instructed us to "fight the good fight of faith." we are NOT pacifists; we are NOT here on earth to just defend ourselves. **We are to engage the enemy; to take the offensive.** We have BOTH a commission and a mandate from our Lord.

PRINCIPLES OF ENGAGEMENT
PRINCIPLE #10

PRINCIPLE 10 - THE DIRECTIVE AND MANDATE

The Jewish Messiah, the Lord from Heaven, made the Directive plain, and He also told what would be the concomitant result.

"And you shall receive power, after the Holy Spirit has supervened upon you, and you shall be witnesses about me both in Jerusalem, and in all the Palestine areas of Judah, and in the Palestine area of Samaria, and to the farthest places of the world." [Acts 1:8]

"And this good news of the kingdom shall be preached in all the world for a witness unto all nations; and then shall the end have arrived." [Mark 24:14]

The world for "**end**" used in the above verse is the Greek word "**telos**" which means "**the point aimed at as a limit, the termination of an act.**" The primary root of the word is "**tello**" meaning "**to set out for a definite point or goal.**"

Acts 1:8 is BOTH a "directive" and a mandate! A directive and a mandate are BOTH official orders or authoritative instructions; however, **a mandate is more precise and encompassing in that it entails the authority to carry out a policy or act in a certain way . . . and . . . it is a commission to administer a territory!**

The purpose of this section is to cause you to SUCCEED in carrying out the mandate of our Lord Jesus, but also to give you INSIGHT and IDEAS which will enable you to more effectively and expeditiously administer territories and bring about the end result.

Great goals, especially God-given ones, will always cause you to OBTAIN and CONQUER. The Master commissioned us to go into ALL the world. Even though there are tribal and ethnic groups remaining to be reached, plans are now being made by key mission strategists and organizations to reach the remaining ones. Prayer and fasting by faithful prayer warriors will solidify the effort and ensure the success.

For example, Global Prayer Digest at the U.S. Center for World Mission in Pasadena, California, reports the baptism of 1,000 Muslim converts in East Africa. An "unnamed" missionary from one East African country was invited to a rural area to witness this very special event. Another tribe in this area, whose members were formerly animistic, first heard about Christ 25 years ago and became Christians.

Two years before this they were building a large stone church for their village when halfway through the construction, God told them to stop building and go plant churches on their enemy's territory! This enemy tribe was Muslim, and the two groups hated each other to the point where they were killing one another. *"But I say to you who hear, love your enemies, do good to those who hate you."* [Luke 6:27]

As these Christians trusted God and went to their Muslim neighbors, they found God had prepared the hearts of their enemies and they were ready to listen. In fact, **God confirmed His truth for the Muslims with VISIONS and DREAMS about the very things the Christians were telling them**. Now, two years later 1,000 Muslim "enemies" were being baptized into the family of God. The original believers church remains unfinished as a testimony to the tribe's obedience and God's faithfulness.

Years ago there was a whole community of Muslims in Eastern Europe where all the accountable people were born again **in ONE NIGHT when the Lord Jesus appeared to them in DREAMS and VISIONS**. The reason for this was that PRAYER and FASTING had been carried out for over 20 years by a group of people whose relatives had been killed by the people in the Muslim community.

Will you be a faithful PRAYER WARRIOR, who through PRAYER and FASTING will solidify the directive and ensure the success of the mandate by the Master?

While we are reaching our home fronts and other ethnic people and nations around the world, we need to go BACK to Jerusalem. If we are going to reach the masses of Islam, Hindus, and Buddhists, we need to reach out to the Jews. Why? Because God's blessing always spills over FROM the Jewish cup to bless the Gentiles. **Allow me to present two (2) scenarios**:

Scenario 1 - When we reach out to evangelize Israel or the Jews, God will bless us in a unique way and reward us with a greater anointing to reach other people. For the last almost 50 years, whenever I have worked on new projects for the Lord--whether direct ministry or through media--I have attempted to somehow reach out to the Jews and/or Israel. Because of this, there was always a great anointing from the Holy Spirit upon the projects, as well as personal and spiritual blessing … PLUS rewards!

Scenario 2 – The Jews have historically been leaders, and gifted in the respective fields of medicine and science, theater, education, creative arts, literature, and business. They have been given a "talent" for making wealth. They have been granted a divine vigor, force, or capacity for getting wealth.

"But you shall remember the LORD thy God: for it is He that gives you power to get wealth, that He may establish his covenant which he swore unto your fathers, as it is this day." [Deuteronomy 8:18]

The Hebrew word for "**wealth**" in the above verse is "**chayil**" which means "**a force, whether of men, means or other resources: an army, wealth, virtue, valor, strength, goods, riches**."

➡ What a resource of wealth and genius that can be anointed by the Ruach Elohim, the Spirit of God, to publish the Good News in every region, to help spiritually administer the territories for Yeshua, and to bring about the end result: the return of Messiah and the literal establishment of His Kingdom on Planet Earth.

By 2024 the world population is estimated to be eight (8) Billion. By 2030 India is expected to surpass China as having the largest population in the world. In 2014 37percent of the world's population lived in India and China combined. At this time, China is first in world trade.

HOW TO SUCCESSFULLY

COMPLETE THE MANDATE

Will you be a faithful PRAYER WARRIOR, who through PRAYER and FASTING will solidify the directive and ensure the success of the mandate by the Master?

Will you FAST and PRAY for Buddhist, Islamic, and Hindu regions to be inundated with the Spirit and for whole REGIONS and KEY people to be visited by the Lord Jesus in person, or in dreams and visions?

Will you reach out in WITNESS and in PRAYERS and FASTING for Jews and for Israel?

Right NOW, there are thousands of young Chinese Christians who have vowed and given their lives to reach Islamic nations. There are KEY Chinese leaders (many who have been tortured, persecuted, and imprisoned) who are planning to go to ALL the nations on their way BACK to JERUSALEM! I have been with some of them ... and they are serious unto the death.

They have already been prepared and refined in the furnace of the Master! **Don't think negatively: *"There are so many Buddhists and Muslims in the world!"*** God did NOT say: "The world would be filled with Muslims, Hindus, and Buddhists." God said: *"But as truly as I live, all the earth will be filled with the glory of the LORD."* [Numbers 14:21]

DISCUSSION GROUP

If you are a ministry leader, will you TARGET India, China, Islamic and Jewish areas of your community and the world through means of the following resources:

☞ Plan Spirit designed MINISTRY or MEDIA projects to reach these areas.

☞ PRAY and FAST for these areas; RECRUIT systematic prayer and fasting for these areas from the people you lead and with whom you are associated.

☞ Include ministry to JEWS and ISRAEL in your projects as the Holy Spirit leads you.

In these last days the DIRECTIVE and MANDATE are coming about "full circle." We are living in the time of the end. **Back to Jerusalem** on the way through the Gentile nations.

PRINCIPLES OF ENGAGEMENT
PRINCIPLE #11

PRINCIPLE 11 - SUDDEN SHOCK

In Principle #9 we discussed in detail "Security and Intelligence." For SUDDEN SHOCK to be effective, the enemy's force must NOT be aware of our plans. They must have NO information of the following:

- WHAT we will do;

- WHEN we will do it; and,

- WHERE we will do it.

These are the only three (3) components (or a combination of them) with which we may use to our advantage the principle of sudden shock ... and to the great disadvantage of the enemy.

The success of sudden shock depends greatly upon the following:

- The enemy's lack of knowledge of your plans.

- Your information concerning the enemy's schedule, location, and activities.

The Japanese attack on Pearl Harbor which started World War II was aided by ignorance on the part of the USA. So was Gideon's attack on the enemy aided by ignorance on the part of the Midianites [Judges Chapter 7].

It is imperative that you keep your plans, strategies, and purposes secret. They must be confidential.

The decision to fight--and the surprise attack—both are caused by YOU. If your friends, family, neighbors, or other people were subjugated by an enemy ... and if you had the POWER to rescue and deliver them ... wouldn't you do it? How much more in the spiritual realm, which has to do with BOTH deliverance and blessing! We should be agents of rescue and deliverance to people here on Planet Earth, and at the same time bringing them eternal benefits.

In certain types of evangelism we must keep our plans and strategies secret. Surely this does NOT apply to events where we want large crowds to attend; that is, where we will be inviting people. However, in many outreaches, especially cross-cultural ones, we must take advantage of the element of SUDDEN SHOCK.

THINK ABOUT IT

What are some ways you could use **sudden shock** to evangelize:

     In mass evangelism?

     In personal evangelism?

Brainstorm with you planning group.

➡ God is never taken by shock. The devil, on the other hand, has been terminally wounded by the element of sudden shock. **He even was used to bring about his own defeat through unintelligence** (the lack of knowledge of strategy) ... AND ... sudden shock:

"Which none of the princes of this world knew: for had they known it, they would not have crucified the Lord of glory." [1 Corinthians 2:8]

When the demonic forces used **both** Herod (the Gentiles) **and** the Jews to crucify Jesus, they did not know that would bring about their demise and the defeat of Satan. Jesus' death and the BLOOD He shed on the cross, paid for the sins of man, and healed the separation between mankind and God. It defeated and broke the bondage of Satan so that men could be free.

God has infinite strategies to help you as a warrior; just spend time with the Holy Spirit and listen! Your Commander has ordered the victory and given you the weapons you need. Now . . . take the offensive, move in faith, possess the territory, and drive out the enemy.

Commander of the army of the LORD be with you.
[Tanakh: Joshua 5:13-15]

QUESTION

HAVE YOU CHOSEN WARRIORS THAT CAN KEEP YOUR PLANS SECRET?

PRINCIPLES OF ENGAGEMENT PRINCIPLE #12

PRINCIPLE #12 - NETWORKING IN UNITY

Many times daily, and always weekly, I am able to network with people in different countries to bring the

Good News to people. By working with others you can greatly multiply your productivity in the Spirit.

The Lord taught me the value of unity as a young minister when I lived and preached on the streets of a large metropolitan city. There were people from many Christian denominations, and some from none, who were there evangelizing. Whenever there was persecution on danger, it was not hard for the Christians to band together. How much more should that be true and operative in the larger war against Satan and his forces.

To help you achieve this principle of "Networking in Unity" **I am going to share with you eight (8) principles the Holy Spirit wants you to know.** They will help you to know how to work with other Christians.

"Behold, how good and how pleasant it is for brethren to dwell together in unity. It is like the precious ointment upon the head, that ran down the beard even Aaron's beard: that went down to the skirts of his garments; As the dew of Hermon, and as the dew that descended upon the mountains of Zion: for there the Lord commanded the blessing, even life forevermore." [Psalm 133:1-3]

Dew is soft and fresh every morning. It cleanses and makes things pleasant. It aids growth and beauty!

"Endeavoring to keep the unity of the Spirit in the bond of peace." [Ephesians 4:3]

Unity is good and pleasant!

To make sure that God's blessings flow freely, that the gifts of the Spirit operate in a pure fashion, and that church growth is at a maximum, we must do our best to promote and maintain UNITY among believers: internally and externally.

Internally, among the members of our own fellowship; and, externally, among all believers (Christians from other churches and fellowships). It takes work (endeavoring) to promote and maintain unity. There are several sub-principles involved in promoting and maintaining unity.

- The Abrahamic Principle

- The Bridge Principle

- The Servant Principle

- The Power Principle

- The Oneness Principle

- The Glory Principle

- The Cell Division Principle

- The Responsibility Principle

THE ABRAHAMIC PRINCIPLE

"There was a strife between the herdsmen of Abram's cattle and the herdsmen of Lot's cattle ... and Abram said unto Lot, 'Let there be no strife I pray thee, between me and thee, and between my herdsmen and thy herdsmen, for we be brethren. Is not the whole land before thee? Separate thyself, I pray thee, from me: if you will take the left hand, then I will go to the right; or if you depart to the right hand; then I will go to the left'." [Genesis 13:7-9]

70

Abram's nephew, Lot, had been blessed greatly just because he was in Abraham's family and under the blessing of Abraham. [Genesis 12:1-3] Lot's herds of cattle had grown in number to the extent that the land was too small for both Lot's and Abram's herds. Their herdsmen were fighting.

Abram had every right to ask ... or even demand ... that Lot and his herdsmen depart to another place; however, Abram let Lot choose which land he wanted. "If you depart to the right hand, then I will depart to the left." [Genesis 13:9] After Lot had separated from him, the Lord said unto Abram, *"For all the land which you see, to thee will I give it, and to thy descendants forever."* [Genesis 13:15]

If the Lord doesn't tell you to maintain control of a position then there's nothing wrong with backing up in the spirit of Christ and releasing a position to maintain unity. [Matthew 5:38-48] I personally know of a situation that happened several years ago in a church where two ministers were co-pastoring.

The older pastor was well-known around the world as a Christian speaker and author. The younger pastor was seemingly mature for his age. The older people in the church sided with the younger pastor while the younger people sided with the older pastor.

Things became so bad to where one day the police were called to the church to stop quarreling and arguing. One of the two groups had actually locked the other group of people out. This was a shame, as well as a reproach on the Body of Christ, and resulted in a lengthy article (with photos) appearing in the newspaper.

Previously, this church had been at the forefront of a move of God's Spirit in this area and community. Now ... it had become a reproach. People had come from distances to be healed, saved, and baptized in the Holy Spirit. It was previously a holy testimony in a large area surrounded by three cities. After the scandal mentioned above people were ashamed to go there.

I had attended this church a few times before. There had always been a sweet presence of God's Spirit; however, I attended once before the incident described above. **I left during the service because the anointing of God was not there**. I knew nothing of the problem(s) they were having.

All that would have had to happen to preserve the testimony of God in this church ... and to make sure God's blessings continued to flow freely ... was for one of the co-pastors to back-up (as Abraham did with Lot) and relinquish / release the pastorship to the other. Even if one of the pastors would have left willingly and permanently for the sake of Christ (to maintain unity), God would have blessed him greatly. The way it was, both pastors left in shame and the move of the Spirit was quenched.

Note: Personally, I do not think it is a good idea to have co-pastors. There needs to be an order in the church, and somebody needs to be in charge. This does NOT mean there cannot be several pastors under one senior pastor.

THE BRIDGE PRINCIPLE

Paul and Barnabas made many disciples in several cities and ordained elders. They "returned again ..." [Acts 14:21]

There is an old saying, "Build bridges ... don't burn them!" Some people break off relationships permanently without allowing time for God to bring healing ... or without "forgiving". **Any wise military leader knows that sometimes you have to destroy bridges so the enemy cannot cross over them (or use them)**; however, whenever feasible it is best to leave the bridges for your ground troops to utilize ... or you will have to build new ones.

As in football, basketball, baseball, rugby, or any sport **... your best defense is a good offense! Build relationships with other people and ministries ... don't burn them!** Paul was constantly building good, permanent relationships by leading people to Christ and by training them to be disciples and followers of Christ.

Previously we studied *"Keys To Foundational Relationships."* We learned that sometimes it is God's will for us to break off relationships, but that is surely NOT the case all the time! If you, or a Christian brother or sister, have a problem constantly breaking off relationships with people, then ask God for healing.

➡ Usually such problems arise out of insecurity or out of "fear of failure" to handle situations: insecurity that is usually imbedded from childhood; or, "fear of failure" resulting from repeated past negative performance. Also, the problems may occur sometimes because of a bad spirit (a demon) and must be dealt with by prayer, confession of the Word of God, and sometimes counseling with exorcism.

Remember, with Jesus Christ you have a new start everyday. Learn to cultivate good friendships with people in other churches and ministries. Show them ...

and yourself ... that the Holy Spirit lives in you. A very wise man in God's service, and one of my best friends, told me one time, "Show Christians that Jesus Christ can live in someone else, too! That He doesn't just live in them!!"

King Saul was a classic case of a "**bridge-burner**". King David was a classic case of a "**bridge builder**". [1 Samuel Chapters 10 through 31] "Bridge-burning" usually results from insecurity, fear, or jealousy ... or a combination of them; and often manifests with the OLD order trying to "spear" the NEW order to the wall. King Saul was jealous of the anointing from God upon David! He was mad at David and afraid of him because God was with him. [1 Samuel 18:5-12]

Be aware of something: The "new order" does not necessarily mean young in age or seniority ... or inexperienced. The "new order" can be older people ... seasoned, experienced people ... breaking away from established religious form: form that was once fresh with the Spirit.

If we find ourselves in the "old order", we need to build bridges with the "new order" to establish UNITY for the Lord's sake. This will accomplish two things: **1)** It will assure that we are open to what the Spirit is doing; and, **2)** It will place us in a position of blessing (to receive a new anointing and to receive God's best as a "peace-maker" for unity's sake [Matthew 5:9]).

When we pray the suggested guidelines for prayer daily as the Lord suggested (the disciple's prayer [Luke 11:1-4]), we are asking for God's will ... and if we mean what we pray ... we will be open to what God wants and what God does. God wants unity among his people; and God honors "bridge-building". [Ephesians 4:3] To fulfill your ministry you must build bridges!

THE SERVANT PRINCIPLE

True spirituality is seeing a need and meeting it. To minister is to serve! It is not always easy to promote and maintain unity among believers; however, the rewards are fantastic. There are at least three reasons for promoting and maintaining unity among believers:

- It is God's will [Ephesians 4:3]

- It helps multitudes of people [Deuteronomy 32:30]

- It is rewarding to you [Matthew 5:9]

The Scripture tells us to " ... *serve one another in love."* [Galatians 5:13] We are commanded in Ephesians 4:3 to *"make every effort to keep the unity of the Spirit in the binding power of peace."* This is one of the jobs, or tasks, that God assigned us. And, the Holy Bible says, *"Whatever your job [task], work at it heartily as something you do for the Lord and not for men."*

There is a NEED for unity and we are to meet that need! You must have the consciousness or the "mentality" to know that God always wants you to bring unity into situations. Pray for an anointing of unity. Let God use you as an instrument of unity!

THE POWER PRINCIPLE

Leviticus 26:8:

➡ 5>100 = 1>20 / 100>10,000 = 1>100 = **5X**

Deuteronomy 32:30:

➡ 1>1,000 = 1>1,000 / 2>10,000 = 1>5,000 = **5X**

God's miracles, the operations of the gifts of the Spirit, and church growth are all attended by power that works through love. **God is a God of power who loves us!**

One of the principles involved with promoting and maintaining unity is "The Power Principle". If disciples are taught properly, **this principle is self-propagating and allows for advances in God's kingdom by quantum leaps.** Lots of Christians, even church leaders, know about this principle but fail to utilize it to their greatest advantage.

"And five of you shall chase an hundred, and an hundred of you shall put ten thousand to flight: and your enemies shall fall before you by the sword." [Leviticus 26:8]

"How should one chase a thousand, and two put ten thousand to flight, except their Rock had sold them, and the Lord had shut them up?" [Deuteronomy 32:30]

Many leaders will use this principle to an extent-- but not as greatly as they could--because of pride! They will not go beyond the barriers where unity demands humility, forgiveness, or acceptance of brethren outside the fold; that is, outside of their fellowship or doctrine. The mathematical ratios in both Leviticus 26:8 and Deuteronomy 32:30 show that with unity you can do much more: in these cases, five (5) times as much!

For example, in Deuteronomy 32:30, one person can chase 1,000. We would expect by mathematical addition that two would chase two times as much, or 2,000. However, two can chase 10,000 with God's anointing, which is five times as much! The ratios are not what is important ... the fact is: **UNITY produces a multiplication of results!**

For Jesus' sake, and His kingdom's sake, we need to humble ourselves, be willing to forgive, and accept all who are purchased with the blood of Christ. If Jesus bought them with his blood, then we should be willing to fellowship to promote and maintain unity!

THE ONENESS PRINCIPLE

There is an amazing spiritual truth we find in Genesis 11:1-9. Before the nations of the earth were scattered on the face of the earth, the earth was of one language and one speech. The people had decided to make a city and a tower, whose top would reach unto heaven; they wanted to make a name for themselves so they would not be scattered abroad upon the face of the earth.

"And the Lord said, 'Behold, the people is one, and they all have one language; and this they begin to do: and now nothing will be restrained from them, which they have imagined to do." [verse 6]

"Let us go down, and there confound their language, that they may not understand one another's speech." [verse 7]

Archaeological records show us that these were wicked and idolatrous people. Yet we see in verse 6 that God said, "**nothing will be restrained from them**". Notice they had ONE goal and ONE speech. They were unified in purpose and language.

If this principle of "oneness" works in unbelievers ... for ungodly, wicked people--how much more will it work for believers--for God's people who have ONE goal and ONE speech: a common vision and a common language!

➡️Especially spirit-filled Christians who have a common objective and who can pray and decree a thing (or a set of objectives) in not only their common earthly language(s) but also their heavenly language: tongues!

In Job 22:28 we read, *"You shall also decree a thing, and it shall be established unto you ..."* In the original Hebrew language the word "**decree**" is a primitive root form of the word "**gazar**", which means "**to cut out exclusively, or to decide**". In its primitive form it is used also as a "**quarrying**" term ... **as in cutting out stone from a rock quarry**.

It means more than to "say" or "speak". It conveys the meaning of "**cutting something out in your mind's eye**"; that is, "**to envision [to make a vision], to decide upon it, and confess it**" ... and then it will be established unto you!

If you and your Christian brothers and sisters have a common vision or goal, and decide upon it, confessing it in a common language, speaking it ... "nothing will be restrained from you which you have imagined (or, envisioned) to do!! [Read again Genesis 11:1-6.]

THE GLORY PRINCIPLE

In His high priestly prayer for his Father to glorify him [John Chapter 17], Jesus asked the Father that all believers may be one in the Father and the Son so that the world may believe and be convinced that God sent Jesus (to earth).

In other words, the world will KNOW and BELIEVE that God sent Jesus to earth when they SEE Christians in unity!

CAUTION

PRIDE IS ONE OF SATAN'S KEY SPIRIT WEAPONS

DON'T LET PRIDE HINDER OPERATING IN UNITY

Disunity is disruptive to the purpose of God. That is, it interrupts the flow of the Spirit and causes disorder. There are several examples of unity and disunity in the Holy Bible and the results thereof.

EXAMPLES OF UNITY:

Abraham and Lot [Genesis 12:5; 13:1-8]

Ruth and Naomi [Ruth 1:16-17]

Jonathan and David [1 Samuel 18:1-4; 19:1-7; 20:4, 35-42]

Rechabites [Jeremiah 35:2-5, 18]

The Early Church [Acts 2:44-45]

EXAMPLES OF DISUNITY:

- Joseph and brothers [Genesis 37; 42:21-22]

- Shechemites [Judges 9:1-6, 22-52]

- Esau and Jacob [Genesis 25 and 28]

- Jehu and others [2 Kings 9]

- Corinthian believers [1 Corinthians 6:1-8]

Knowing that disunity hinders the work of God and that unity promotes the work of God **we should have a "mind set" to always make a quality decision to promote and maintain unity among believers** ... so the world may believe and be convinced that God sent Jesus to earth! We need to do it for the GLORY of Jesus Christ who did His best for us!!

THE CELL DIVISION PRINCIPLE

The Principle of Cell Division usually results in **church growth**. Disagreements among Christian brethren do not mean they are not spiritual (or, that the brethren are out of God's will); disagreements may mean God is leading them in different directions, or that God has other plans than they have previously considered.

Disagreements may be a sign of transition; and sometimes of great change which will result in quantum leaps: great advances in the Kingdom of God. Disagreements may produce paradigm shifts: patterns, or models, of a new work God is "fathering" in the earth.

In Acts 15:36-41 Paul and Barnabas had an angered dispute; so much so that they departed or split; just as some churches have done. **This does not mean they were out of God's will**. God used Paul and Barnabas each in the separate directions to which He directed them in order to establish and strengthen the church.

The Holy Bible tells us, *"Be ye angry and sin not; let not the sun go down upon your wrath."* [Ephesians 4:26] The Amplified Bible says. *"When angry do not sin; do not ever let your wrath (your exasperation, your fury or indignation) last until the sun goes down. Leave no such room or foothold for the devil (give no opportunity to him)."* [Verses 26 & 27]

THE RESPONSIBILITY PRINCIPLE

You, as a minister of Christ, have a responsibility to do what is right, and never to take part, or be part, of wrong-doing. If you are in a relationship where someone over you in a position of authority is doing wrong, or you feel they are doing something wrong, (or, in error), then you have the responsibility to do what is right.

First, go talk to them. Most of the time, the situation will be worked out. **Lots of times, it is just a matter of communication, or misunderstanding**. However, if the person who is over you in the Lord does not agree with you and continues to do what you feel is wrong, then you need to "back-out" or discontinue the relationship.

➡ Here's why! If the person over you in the Lord is doing wrong, you don't want to be part of their wrong doing; however, if they are right, you don't want to be

81

opposing, or fighting God's will. Peacefully exit the situation. Be responsible!

You are accountable for your actions before God. In 2 Timothy 1:7 we read, *"God did not give us a spirit of fear, but a spirit of power, of love, and of self-discipline (or, sound mind)."* You are morally and spiritually obliged before God to deal with the situation in a mature and responsible way!

You will have God's peace knowing you have acted responsibly in wisdom and rightness--not in emotional anxiety or fear--and for the sake of UNITY you will have made a quality decision!

Now you know the principles for working productively, effectively, and harmoniously with other Christians. You know WHY and HOW the Lord would have you operate with other believers. Follow these principles and you will have plenty of blessings on earth ... and be a channel of blessings to many others. Also, Heaven will reveal to you the extreme fruitfulness of your wise obedience to the Commander of the Forces: the Lord Jesus.

ASSIGNMENT

WRITE DOWN SOME METHODS YOU CAN UTILIZE TO FOSTER UNITY

MAKE PLANS TO PUT THEM INTO ACTION SOON.

PRINCIPLES OF ENGAGEMENT
PRINCIPLES #13 AND #14

PRINCIPLE 13 - REBELLION AGAINST SATAN

Your service for the Great Commander, Lord Jesus, should be based upon your love for Him and thankfulness for what He has done for you. However, as in any war, your hatred for the enemy and his ideology should also motivate you to action. The enemy wanted you--and your family and loved ones--to spend eternity in the Lake of Fire with him; a torment that would never end!

The devil came to steal from you, to kill you, and to destroy you. He wanted--and wants--the worst for you and your family and loved ones. **You should HATE the devil.** Never give him any place to operate in your life or ministry ... or your mind! Rebel against him and all that he stands for.

IDEA

WRITE DOWN ALL THE WAYS SATAN HAS TRIED TO DESTROY YOU

THEN REBEL . . . PLAN AN ATTACK THAT WILL BRING PEOPLE TO CHRIST

PRINCIPLE 14 – LOGISTICS

Logistics has to do with the supply or provision of materials, information, and personnel. No military force can engage the enemy for long if there is a deficiency or interruption in the supply thereof. Napoleon said, "An army marches on its stomach." But, communication, good intelligence, ammunition and armament with other materials--**and the right kind of personnel**--are also imperative if we want to successfully engage the enemy.

To be safe from the enemy we must protect our lines of communication and supply while at the same time intercepting the enemy's lines of communication and supply. In World War II the USA saved itself from defeat in the South Pacific by use of the "Wind Talkers."

These were a valiant group of Native American Navajo Indians. The Navajos had their own mother tongue which the Japanese could not understand. They could not break the code of the Navajos which was key in ordering in air assaults to specific areas and also in communicating other secret information.

In the *Dictionary of U.S. Miliary Terms* **"lines of communication"** is defined as: **"All the routes, land, water, and air which connect an operating military force with its base of operations, along which supplies and reinforcements move."** Many military battles have been lost because of NOT following this principle. The reason is usually because of one of the following:

⚡ By advancing too far or too fast for supplies to keep up; or,

⚡ By allowing an enemy to break through and cut off supplies.

Jewish, Messianic Hebrew, and Christian leaders need to organize [secret] societies for prophetic performance, not only NOW but even more as we prepare to enter into the last days. It will be too late if

84

we wait to attempt the same at that time. And we need to stay in close communication with our Commander-In-Chief: Yeshua, the Messiah.

In these societies we need to have brothers and sisters who are tradesmen, skilled craftsmen, businessmen, bankers, builders, economists, ministers, doctors, suppliers, and any who have a like vision for networking to not only help each other but to work together in unity to provide for Messianic evangelism and discipleship, along with synagogue and church planting ... and **to provide for logistical needs in the Body of Messiah.**

➡ Also, **there needs to be networking of those who are skilled in cyber warfare and hacking**: not only for protection for the People of God from Evil Empires---synagogues and real churches may be underground in the future---but also for **intelligence gathering and communication of the Word of the LORD to the masses**. Communication to the mass of the populace can effected pro-actively by hacking into key centers of communication with:

     The Good News of Messiah;

     Revelation to the masses about current prophecy being fulfilled in current events;

     Prophetic messages from real modern day Prophets of God.

This revelational communication should increase as we see the Day of Messiah approaching!

As we maintain close fellowship with the Lord, we will be guaranteed the fellowship with others of like mind: **a**

close-knit Spirit-directed group of brethren with like vision.

SUGGESTION

START A SECRET SOCIETY CALLED "APOSTLES OF THE MOST HIGH"

PRINCIPLES OF ENGAGEMENT
PRINCIPLE #15 AND PRINCIPLE MAXIMUS

PRINCIPLE 15 - MANAGEMENT OF RESOURCES

We need to be efficient and effective in warfare, to strike at the decisive point with concentration, but at the same time with good management of resources. It is foolish to have 3,000 Christian workers in one well evangelized country while none, or few, are in a mostly NON Christian area.

Proper mobilization of warriors calls for re-alignment, or re-assessment, of our mission strategies. It is hard to get workers in some places. However, if we are in communication with our Commander-In-Chief, surely He--Who is all knowing--will reveal to us HOW, WHEN, and WHERE to strike. It maybe through:

- The media

- Floating bobbles

- Homing pigeons or birds

- Airplanes dropping literature

- Re-assignment of some warriors

- CD's & DVD's smuggled in with the right language

- Helium balloons filled with Gospel tracts in the right language

- Secret publishing and distribution centers in underground churches

- Hacking into public, private, educational and governmental media outlets to preach the Good News

- Other ideas: *Using the Media to Proclaim the Good News.* You may access this teaching at www.apostle.libsyn.com. (It is located in the *Archives*: August 13, 2013.)

Gideon used pitchers and candles. **We must not keep picking the harvest on the front row while nobody is planting seeds on the back row.** And, always plan for follow-up when and if possible.

Good management of resources directs and uses the people and materials available to **take the OFFENSIVE and strike** at DECISIVE POINTS with concentration, surprise, and mobility. **We need flexible warriors who can move quickly and are "cross trained" to work in multi-cultural and multi-language environments.** For example: a Masei, Turkana, or Samburu person should be well supplied and supported to reach the nomadic peoples of East Africa; not to be spending time evangelizing the Irish (unless the Holy Spirit directs).

It doesn't take a Christian from a nomadic background nearly as much money to live as a Christian worker in another area, so **why not put the money where it reaps the greatest reward, or harvest?** Also, **why not move warriors into position - or locations - for effective military action.** Instead of concentrating warriors in highly Christian areas, move them - and ready them - for CONCENTRATED SURPRISE ASSAULTS at key decisive points. Organize short term mobile units from different areas that can be used for concentrated offensives: temporary assault units. They may go and come from other areas of permanent ministry, or they may come from their normal work for a short period of time.

CHALLENGE

BRAINSTORM WITH YOUR GROUP
PLAN A CREATIVE ASSAULT

USE GOOD MANAGEMENT OF RESOURCES
PRAY FOR CREATIVITY

DON'T FORGET TO PROVIDE
FOR UNIQUE FOLLOWUP

Leaders and pastors, especially of apostolic churches and ministry in these last days, need to plan economically viable strategies of warfare: how much of what - and whom - goes where! This is NOT a play game in which we are involved: this is WAR . . . and we must be "a lean, clean fighting machine" fit for the Masters use!

Gideon used excellent management of resources because he listened to God. He used less than one percent [<1%] of his military force. He sent 22,000 fearful people home, another 9,700 that weren't ready, and fought with only 300 of the original 32,000. [Judges Chapter 7 and 8]

Establish prayer groups **whose ONLY job is to pray for warriors.** *"The harvest is abundant, but the reapers are few; therefore entreat the Owner of the harvest to send out more reapers into His fields."* [Luke 10:2, Weymouth New Testament]

PRINCIPLE MAXIMUS

In addition to the 15 principles discussed previously in the Principles of Engagement, there is one other principle that I call "Principle Maximus" and **it is VITAL to the total annihilation of the enemy: our maximum victory.** I will discuss it here.

A defeated enemy, as they are retreating and running, is dangerous. They will fight to the death many times. They will destroy infrastructure: roads, bridges, utilities, farms.

Total annihilation of the enemy is mandatory ... it is necessary! The winning army, including the leadership, has a temptation to relax: to go for rest and recreation. This is NOT the time. The enemy must be completely destroyed.

Do NOT give the enemy time to regroup. In the Christian parallel the final consummation of the victory, and it MUST be accomplished, is: 1. Followup of new converts; 2. Growing disciples; and, 3. Planting new churches. This is vital. Give the enemy NO place, no base, from which to operate.

When a person comes to Christ, then **provide them with ALL the teaching they can, or desire to, receive**.

➡ Teach them about salvation, healing, the baptism in the Holy Spirit, prosperity, how to hear from God, how to start a church, the end times and the return of Christ ... plus prophecy. **Salvation is just the start! God's program involves deliverance and enlargement**.

QUESTIONS

**ARE THERE SOME BATTLES
YOU HAVE NOT COMPLETED**

**IS IT FEASIBLE TO CORRECT
AND RE-ATTACK**

TOOLS FOR DISCIPLES AND CHURCH GROWTH

At The University of Excellence we provide FREE Bible Studies: to take the new convert through the New Testament ... so that Messiah and His Word will be formed in their hearts. Also, to teach them about the last days. From experience through the years, I have found that **when people learn about the End Times and God's program for the last days, they grow as disciples** and become stronger witnesses. These studies **plus Rabbinical Studies** are available at: www.marketplaceworld.com. (Select *Study Materials*.)

- French Bible Studies

- Spanish Bible Studies

- English Bible Studies

- Rabbinical Studies

Also, to help in church planting and discipleship development there are 1,000's of teachings available through the resources at: **www.princehandley.com**. It is a "portal" of many websites and podcast sites and other resources where **many people have received salvation, miracles, healing and spiritual growth**.

And, for strategic planning---both in missions and self-development---there are Prince Handley Books: **to bring relevant, cutting edge teaching** in **both e-Book and print format**. Teaching to help disciples **develop** and to help them to **receive MIRACLES** through the medium of the printed word. (See list on back page.)

➡ **You must follow up . . . otherwise you are giving the enemy an opportunity to regroup.**

Look at the example of Gideon. He and his 300 men had killed 120,000 of the enemy. However, he didn't stop there. There were only 15,000 of the enemy left. Gideon and his men were hungry and weary. Yet, Gideon went on and pursued the enemy. Gideon called for the men he had previously sent home. The enemy, and the two enemy king leaders, were totally defeated. After that, Gideon returned.

ASSIGNMENT

PLAN A COMPLETE BATTLE OBJECTIVE
(INCLUDING FOLLOWUP)

After the great breakthrough of the offensive, after striking at the decisive points and experiencing victory, **then it is time to follow up** with:

- Literature programs;

  - Media blitzes;

  - Bible studies and discipleship;

  - Home prayer and study groups;

  - Schools of ministry (behind every bush);

  - Start Churches and Messianic Synagogues;

  - Apostles sent out;

  - Ministry of helps: to orphans and fatherless, widows, the hungry; and,

  - Healing rooms and prayer centers in cities and villages.

Act on your thoughts and instincts. **Lift up your vision.** Finish the work you've been assigned. The Mashiach of Israel is waiting!

Operating in the principles we have discussed in this book AND utilizing Principle Maximus will assure you of this commendation from the Commander of the Army of the LORD:

Well done!

You are a good and faithful servant!

Enter into the JOY of the Lord.

LIVE A LIFE OF EXCELLENCE!

Prince Handley

✦ ✦ ✦

NOTICE

Look for the companion book in the *Missions Series* by Prince Handley titled, **New Global Strategy**. Available at Amazon and other fine book stores.

Email prayer requests and praise reports to:
princehandley@gmail.com

Or write to:
Prince Handley
P.O. Box A
Downey, California 90241 USA

UNIVERSITY OF EXCELLENCE PRESS

NOTE

We listen to our readers. Tell us what **new** subject matter you would like to see published. Email your ideas to: universityofexcellence@gmail.com.

OTHER BOOKS BY PRINCE HANDLEY
CLICK ON THE LINKS BELOW

🖝 Map of the End Times

🖝 How to Do Great Works

🖝 Flow Chart of Revelation

🖝 Action Keys for Success

🖝 Health and Healing Complete Guide to Wholeness

🖝 Prophetic Calendar for Israel and the Nations: The Next Decade (2014 – 2023)

🖝 Healing Deliverance

🖝 How to Receive God's Power with Gifts of the Spirit

🖝 Healing for Mental and Physical Abuse

🖝 Victory Over Opposition and Resistance

🖝 Healing of Emotional Wounds

🖝 How to Be Healed and Live in Divine Health

🖝 Healing from Fear, Shame and Anger

🖝 How to Receive Healing and Bring Healing to Others

🖝 New Global Strategy: Enabling Missions

AVAILABLE AT AMAZON AND OTHER BOOK STORES
UNIVERSITY OF EXCELLENCE PRESS

www.ingramcontent.com/pod-product-compliance
Lightning Source LLC
Chambersburg PA
CBHW070540030426
42337CB00016B/2281